The Emotion, The Tree and Me:

A Guide To Discussing Emotional Health and Wellness With Your Children.

Chase Martin Moore

Printed in the United States of America

10 9 8 7 6 5 4 3 2

EMPIRE PUBLISHING

www.empirebookpublishing.com

Contents

About the Author... 1

Introduction 3

Chapter 1

Knowing and Growing Your Roots.. 5

Chapter 2

Learning the Ways of the Weather 33

Chapter 3

Big and Beautiful Like Me... 59

Chapter 4

Teaching Points and Critical Conversations............................... 65

Utilizing this Book

Social and Emotional Learning (SEL) enhances the capacity of our youth to connect with others and develop a healthy relationship with themselves (intrapersonal skills), as well as accurately perceive the world, so they can manage behaviors and deal effectively and ethically with life. This book will support you and your family to cultivate social-emotional skills.

The contents of this work are designed to increase social-emotional functioning through developing knowledge of one's culture, one's family, and ultimately one's self as it is the belief of the author that you cannot truly achieve wellness without a firm understanding of yourself. Further, you cannot honestly know yourself until you know the ones who are closest to you. Through this book, we will listen to a story and develop common emotional language so that we create a multigenerational conversation regarding mental health, wellness, and emotional intelligence. The author explores five core competencies through this book as our children must be exposed to and reach social-emotional milestones related to Self-Awareness, Self-Management, Social Awareness, Relationship Skills, and Responsible decision making.

Through this book, you and your student(s) can utilize the story and its accompanying informational guide to learn and answer questions that will teach and promote growth in the five critical anchors standards for social-emotional learning. This book is designed to provide a head start for parents, caring adults, and teachers who seek to increase the social and emotional competence of the children and youth in their lives.

Please take the time and read through the story as well as the accompanying informational guide. Social-Emotional Learning differs from academic learning as the best teachers of social-emotional competence are the parents and caring adults in a child's life. Often parents and their children share genetic as well as daily and historical experiences, so there is no one better to teach the social-emotional skills needed to navigate life than the ones closest to you. This book allows students to get to know the adults who have such an influence on their lives.

"You cannot truly know yourself until you truly know the people who raised you."

Resources:

Goals and guidelines for parents and teachers: At the end of each chapter will be goals and standards that can be utilized to guide the development of children/youth. Each benchmark can be expanded and used as a conversation or goal to strengthen mindfulness, mental wellness, and cultural understanding.

Information Guide and Critical Conversations: At the end of each story chapter, you will find author notes entitled Information Guide and Critical Conversations. This section provides the author's professional analysis of key mental health standards as well as research on child/youth development, designed to inform and inspire conversation and learning about mental health. The information and discussion prompts are aligned with social-emotional standards to ensure that the dialogue is teaching developmentally appropriate lessons and providing culturally competent mental health instructions.

Dedication

The dedication of this book goes to my wife and three beautiful children. They have supported me and loved me while I pursue my passion for inspiring and assisting others on their journey for mental wellness. I love you and appreciate all that you do for me. I hope that my actions make you proud to have me as a father and husband. I would also like to send thanks to God, my parents, extended family, and all the elders in my life for cultivating a supportive environment and enriching my life through your experience and wisdom. Without the knowledge and experiences you have provided me with, I would not be in a place to improve the lives of others.

Thank you.

About the Author

Chase Martin Moore is a husband, father of 3, Psychologist, and founder of the Pan African Wellness Center. Chase has spent much of his professional career providing psychological services to students in the K-12 school system. Chase has also served as a school principal and Behavior Analyst, providing behavioral health services to families with special needs students. He is a proud graduate of California State University, Fresno, where he was a collegiate baseball player and earned his bachelor's in psychology. Upon graduation, he attended California State University, Sacramento, as well as Grand Canyon University, where he obtained his Master's degree in School Psychology and Doctorate in Behavioral Health, respectively. Through it all, God and his family have been a constant source of strength and motivation.

Introduction

As a parent of three children, I know that all parents want their children to have a healthy Mindset. That is, we want them to have the mental ability to interpret the world accurately, respond to life situations gracefully, and manage their relationships with themselves and others without stress or strife.

Having a healthy way of organizing and structuring the world allows our children to be prepared for opportunities, have healthy relationships with friends and family, and not be limited by psychopathology that makes them dysfunctional in one or many areas of their life. We want their minds to be like good soil, meaning that it's healthy and fertile enough to produce whatever they desire. Unfortunately, due to our human nature, we can experience challenges that hinder our mental wellbeing. These challenges can come from our environment, our genetics, our habits, and the lack of correct information. No matter what your situation is, you and your family have the responsibility to understand it and make it functional. As parents, we know our children and their environment best, so, understandably, we are in the best position to teach the mental health skills, help them form the mental health habits and structure an environment that cultivates mental wellness.

Through this book, parents will be able to communicate, teach, and learn with their children using a story designed to create common emotional language and imagery to bridge the gap between parents and their children. This book explores how we, as parents, educators, and community mentors to children, can help build their brains and shape the minds of our children as they grow through the different developmental stages. I encourage you and your family to read the stories, have critical conversations, and use the resources provided for you.

As a school psychologist, I know that well-adjusted children do not come from families with perfect lives. They come from families who understand who they are, communicate regularly, love often, and use the social-emotional skills necessary to maintain healthy relationships with their children as they grow through the developmental stages. It is my sincere hope that this book brings you and your family joy, knowledge, and empowerment.

"The best thing you can do for others is to love yourself, understand yourself, work on yourself, and be yourself. As the world needs YOU."

Chase Moore

Chapter 1

Knowing and Growing Your Roots

Social-Emotional Standards Targeted: Self Awareness, Self-Knowledge, Self-Management

Rhea's parents wanted to grow a tree. A tree that would spread beautiful light and energy across the ocean and Sea.

They took the seed to the forest to grow big and tall. They wanted the seed to grow taller than them all.

Just as they planted the seed at the perfect peak. They heard a beautiful
voice that began to speak.

As they looked up to see what it could be, they saw a beautiful tree
standing tall and free.

The tree said,
"I know why you are here; you don't have to tell me.
You want to grow a tree that is big and beautiful like me."

The parents agreed and confirmed that fact they wanted a tree with that
type of impact.

The tree explained "It's important to remember a big beautiful tree like me is not just timber.

I have roots, roots that still grow and they are affected by my emotions, each and every one that I show."

The tree went on and as she explained she told the parents about 4 major roots they must maintain.

Love is a root and Affection is one too. And don't forget about Trust and Reciprocity for you.

These are all important for my foundation and they make me strong and if you keep them safe nothing will go wrong.

The tree said,
"Love is important, and if your tree is going to be free, it must love itself, and then extend that love to you and me.
Trees must learn to trust as this gives us Hope and when we share our trust this helps us Cope.

Coping is important as storms do pass through, but when you have strong roots, storms will not be able to move you.

Coping teaches your tree, how to bend, but never break, for when you have love, there is not a storm you can't take.
This is all possible and destine to be,
but you have to protect the roots, if healthy growth is what you want to see.
Unprotected roots can cause major problems you see,
if you don't develop healthy feelings of love, hope and trust, life may not be easy.

Not trusting people will cause you to push others away,
and having no hope will make you give up before you reach the end of
the day.

As a tree we go through many seasons, and sometimes bad weather hits
us, and we don't always know the reason."

"You will have to teach your tree how to deal with bad weather, as there
will be tough times on life's endeavor.

Anger, sadness, grief and jealousy too, all these emotions can try to take
control of you."

At the end of the day, the parents just had to know,
"What are the things that would NOT make our tree grow?"

The tree said,
"Good things are the sun; learning is the rain, but keep the seed from too
much darkness because that is the pain.
Your seed needs sun and your seed needs rain, darkness is inevitable, but
teach skills to avoid extended pain.
If you can provide these things, your seed is destined to be, as big and as
beautiful, as what you see in me."

In the days to come, the seed would see,
that her mother and father provided reciprocity.

They hugged, they kissed, and attended to every need.
And would you know, the roots were growing strong, indeed.

The roots were growing, oh wow were they strong and just before you
knew it something else came along.

Part 2

Goals and Guidelines for developing strong emotional roots for Ages 7 through 11:

Cultural and Emotional Root system.

1. Recognize that thoughts are frequent but are not always truthful and just because they can create physical sensations does not mean they are true.
2. Recognize the emotional states of people in your home or on a visit to friends and family homes. Have discussions to increase insight into how that affects their behavior.
3. Pick a time when you are calm and identify what balance/calm feels like. Have a discussion about how you can return to balance when you become overly emotional.
4. Select a favorite movie or song and describe a time you felt the same way a story character felt.

Recognize cultural qualities and external supports.

1. Discuss activities that bring you joy, contentment or excitement that you can do with others.
2. Reflect on your home culture as well as ethnic or religious culture and identify the values that help you make good choices or guide your thoughts and behavior.
3. Identify reliable adults from the home, school and community that you would allow to support you during a tough time. Reflect on why you selected these individuals.
4. Describe both positive and negative messages you receive about yourself from your family and friends.

Teaching Points and Critical Conversations:

Roots

Our deeply held beliefs about ourselves, private thoughts, and our habits are all valuable parts of our mental health, and they form the core of our wellness. Through our interactions with people close to us like parents, siblings, and community members, we begin to form and shape our core beliefs, our self-talk, and our habits. We must learn and understand the experiences of those who love us as well as those who influence us. This information gives us insight into how their interactions with us have shaped our thoughts, habits, and behaviors.

We cannot honestly know ourselves until we truly know those who influence us. For example, if in our story Rhea's mother was suffering from severe anxiety, many of their interactions would be based on fear or occur while in a fearful state. Over time, these types of interactions may promote anxiety or anxious behavior in Rhea as people learn what they live and experience. This is because our experiences live not only in our minds, but in our bodies and nervous systems. As humans we regulate our minds and bodies to the energy of the people closest to us. So, our bodies will be wired in a similar manner to those who are consistently in our environment.

Further, if Rhea's father is working long hours, has a sick parent and is in constant fear that he is not performing well at work, he may be bringing home emotional energy that causes him to be short tempered, be harsh or critical and have little energy for family activities. Over time these types of interactions may result in the child developing thoughts, habits and emotions that come from the pain and energy the father has brought to the home. When we know and have insight into the people around us, we can thrive even if our environment is not entirely healthy.

When we learn that our parents and the adults in our lives have their own lives and experiences, we gain insight, understanding, and self-

11

knowledge as we understand why they behave or understand the world as they do.

Knowing your roots and having conversations with the people who are influential in your life can help shape the stories you have created about yourself as these stories affect your self-talk, core beliefs, habits, and the way you see the world. Since no one is perfect, families must discuss their interactions and what may be influencing their communication with each other. Every day we all have experiences that other people are not privy to, and we carry those emotions from the many interactions we have every day. These emotions often are released in the relationships with the people closest to us. Having conversations with family members about their experiences, whether historically or present-day, can create understanding.

For example, If Rhea's family were able to have conversations regarding the experiences they were having, it may create more opportunity for understanding and possibly prevent Rhea from creating negative stories about herself, or from developing habits and behaviors that come from feeling isolated or unloved. It would be important for Rhea to know about the experiences of her family as if she did, she would understand why they behaved towards her the way they did and she could consciously choose how to respond or think about the situation.

When we have conversations with our family about our experiences and how those experiences might affect our interactions with them, we are choosing to heal, and healing can be painful. This is important as many times people confuse pain with trauma. Not everything you experience that is emotionally painful, is traumatic. Some forms of pain are necessary and required for growth and healing. As families we have to choose to address our challenges in a clean and healthy manner.

In all families we have situations that can be painful. Things like parents divorcing, abuse, mental illness or poverty can be hard for families to discuss, challenge and heal. Even stressors like learning disabilities, parent and child disagreements and unrealistic expectations can be painful and have long term effects. However, it's important that families attempt to address these challenges as whether we know it or not it will continue to affect us and those we love. Pain can be transferred from one person to another unknowingly. Just like when you throw a rock in a lake, the ripples from the rock will move far beyond the space it hit in the water. When we choose to ignore challenges in our family both present and past without a willingness to confront our pain, we are refusing to heal. This is why many families have generations of people who experience similar challenges as their ancestors. They pass the pain or personality traits derived from pain to the people they care about unknowingly, through the energy they carry with them. This refusal to repair may save us from some discomfort early on as I know it is much easier to ignore negative, violent or disruptive behavior than to challenge and or attempt to heal it. However, as time goes by, refusal to improve is always more painful than choosing to heal.

This is where the concepts of "clean pain and "dirty pain" come from. "Dirty pain is the pain of avoidance, blame and denial" and "clean pain is pain that mends, builds your capacity for growth and is designed to restore balance through honesty and truth". As you can see, both are still some form of pain because healing hurts! It can be very uncomfortable, and it is certainly work. Families or people who choose not to deal with their pain attempt to heal their pain through ways that ultimately hurt others such as lying, stealing, behaving in manners that are immoral, unloving and are not aligned with healthy values. This would be considered "dirty pain" as it's not life preserving and serves as a foundation for future pain, lies and distortion.

Over time trauma, pain, anger and a lack of healing can lead to a breakdown of the moral, ethical and cultural fabric of our families. When this happens, it can leave individuals and families vulnerable to ideas, behavior orientations and beliefs that are distant from a family's core values. When we heal hurt and become accustomed to clean pain, it allows families to preserve a healthy lifestyle as they learn to work through difficult times as oppose to giving in to them for fear of conflict.

Here is an opportunity to practice using clean pain and honestly assess the perceptions of the children close to you. Below are the seven items on the positive childhood experience (PCE) psychometric analysis that can guide families about the experiences the youth are having in their homes. Please have the children or youth in the home answer (Y) for yes and (N) for no. It's important to remember that the answers are meant to encourage conversation and growth, not blame and resentment. Remember that this is feedback based on perception, and just as we receive feedback every day from our smart watches, our supervisors, and the world, we should accept the input of those we have influence over.

(1) I can talk with my family members about my feelings (Y) (N)

(2) I feel that my family stands by me during difficult times (Y) (N)

(3) The people in my home behave in ways that support my growth and development (Y) (N)

(4) I feel a sense of belonging to my family (Y) (N)

(5) Everyone in my family is treated equally and loved equally (Y) (N)

(6) I feel safe physically and emotionally around everyone I come in contact with (Y) (N)

(7) I can express my deepest thoughts to at least one person in my home. (Y) (N)

(8) The people in my home often show negative emotions such as jealousy, anger, sadness, grief. (Y) (N)

(9) I have exactly what I need in life to be successful, happy and content. (Y) (N)

Authors note: It's not about what you do as parents, it's about what your children perceive. You have to create time to ensure the messages they are receiving from your home environment and interactions with them matches what you intended. As if they perceive:

- If the message they receive from interactions is they are misfortune, they will strengthen roots of self-pity.

- If our perception of reality is that we are constantly belittled, then it will strengthen the roots of insecurity.

- If children witness or experience jealousy, they grow roots of envy.

- If children perceive encouragement, they strengthen the roots of confidence.

- If children perceive tolerance, they strengthen the roots of patience.

- If children perceive praise, they grow appreciation.

- If children perceive they are accepted, they grow love.

Family Discussion Questions: Please read through the questions and answer openly and honestly. Both parents and youth should answer the questions unless it indicates explicitly who the questions are intended for. The questions are designed to provide guidance, information, and instructions for the entire family. Each member of the family must be able to answer freely without interruption. There are no correct answers as the power is in perspective. The questions should be based on how you feel or perceive situations, and accuracy to statements can be addressed at a later time. Please select the questions that are appropriate for you and the people in your life. There is no need for all the questions listed to be asked or answered.

Questions for adults: What present-day or past experiences affect your interactions with your children? What message do you believe your daily interactions with your children send them about their worth and ability?

How do you resolve conflict in your home with your child? Do you think that the current way of resolving conflict leaves a positive message or a negative one?

Critical conversation: What are the beliefs, habits, and rules in your house that seem most important in this discussion? Who decides the rules in your home, and why? Who is responsible for discipline in your home? Who in your home provides emotional support when needed? Do the people in your home consistently have respectful interactions with each other? Do parents and children/youth both receive respect in your home? How do adults show children or youth that they respect them? How is disagreement resolved in your home? Does the process for determining disagreement work for both adults and children/youth?

Ancestors/Family History: Who is a family member that you admire? Why do you admire this person? Is it due to a unique skill or ability that they possess? Who in your family has achieved success based on your family's definition of success? Who has had a difficult time? Why? How well does your family cope with stress? Does your family have a mental health or behavioral history that includes mental illness or other personality character traits that make life difficult?

Culture: How would you describe the culture of which you belong? Does the culture you belong to have specific rules or expectations for behavior, mental, and spiritual health? Do people who share your culture have unique experiences or challenges they must understand? What skills, habits, customs, and norms do your family have that will prepare you for school? Life? Do you have mental health characteristics that come from your culture? Are they positive or negative?

Questions for youth: Who in your life teaches you to manage your emotions? Do you know people in your family who have challenges managing their emotions? How do the adults in your life handle stress? Do you have an emotional challenge that you have experienced or are currently experiencing that you have not told anyone? Do you keep

16

emotional experiences inside because you are afraid of people's reactions? If you told your family about the situations or thoughts that cause you emotional distress do you feel they would react emotionally or stop loving you? What are the forms of stress you experience most frequently? How do you know when people in your home are stressed?

Love

Love is an essential life aspect of wellness and mental health, as it is a vital key in the development of healthy habits. When you love yourself and others in a healthy way, you can act in ways that are supportive of those around you as well as yourself. When you can love yourself, you will discover it is easier to overcome life's obstacles and challenges. Thinking positively about yourself creates good memories, and the positive stories that you will receive from others lead to a belief that you can affect change in your life.

When we value ourselves and know we are deserving of care and concern, it protects us from the daily storms we and others create for ourselves. Self-compassion means treating ourselves the same as we would a friend. Rather than hating, judging, or adding to a friend's despair, we listen with empathy and understanding, to encourage them to remember that mistakes are normal, and validate their emotions without adding fuel to the fire.

When the people in our lives love us in a healthy way, it can give us hope and the support we need to move through life gracefully. Love is an energy that moves us forward and creates healthy thoughts, habits, and actions that lead to success and growth. Not having people who love you in a healthy way can create a lack of self-love, which can make you think or do things that are harmful or unhealthy to yourself. When we perceive that others do not love us in a genuine way or when we experience a type of love that is rooted in selfishness, lust or dependence it hurts our ability to trust others and believe in ourselves. It's important to remember that people can love for many reasons and love by itself is not the ultimate goal. For example, people who abuse drugs can "love" drugs. People who are in relationships can "love" not being alone. However, these are not healthy forms of love.

We need to understand the true definition of love so that we don't get confused when emotional storms come through. Love is much more than a strong feeling of happiness as there are plenty of things that give us happy feelings, and we would not call it love. For example, ice-cream. If you have ever desperately wanted ice cream on a hot day, you were experiencing a strong feeling of like for ice cream. However, we would not say you love ice-cream, and I will tell you why. The critical distinction is that love is not just a good feeling. Instead, love involves responsibility, and there are specific criteria for us to honestly know and use the term love.

The acronym STAR can help you remember all of the criteria for the definition of love:

S) Support: Love involves supporting others and working to help them be the best version of themselves.

Can you think of ways the people in your life who love you, support you? What kind of things do you do for people who you love?

T) Tough: Love is unconditional, and this means that it is stronger than bad behavior, mistakes, or emotion. When you love someone, you love the light inside of them, and even when you can't see their light, you LOVE them enough to use some of your light to brighten theirs.

The above examples are why we would not say you love ice-cream because if your ice-cream cone falls on the dirt, you will not eat it, it's not unconditional, you would not try to piece it back together. However, if someone you love fails a test or loses a game, you do not stop loving them because they are not perfect. This is the difference between love and like. Like, can and often goes away when things change. Love remains the same, no matter what.

Do you feel like the loving relationships with the people in your life are unconditional? Are there times when you feel that a person you love doesn't love you anymore because of something you did wrong?

A) Action: Love involves working to have more positive interactions with someone than negative interactions. Love requires that you behave in a way that is polite, respectful, and thoughtful to a person that you love. This is not saying to be perfect. However, it is valuing the person enough to monitor and ensure you have more positive interactions than negative interactions. Research suggests that we should strive for five positive interactions to every one conflictual interaction.

Do you have people in your life who you love, and you treat with respect, politeness, and thoughtfulness? Are there people in your life that you love, but you are not polite and respectful towards them? If so, why do you think this is?

R) Resilient: Love is resilient; this means that love does not have to be perfect. People we love can make mistakes and we still love them. Love is the freedom to be yourself, and human. Because we are human that means we make mistakes and when someone loves us that means they love us even through our mistakes.

Questions for adults in your life:

1. What is your definition of love?
2. How did the adults in your life show you love?
3. Do you show love to the children in your life the same way adults in your life did? When you are angry with people do you still act in a loving way?
4. Do you feel you love your family in a healthy way? If not, what ways would you improve the way you love your family?

Questions for youth: What have you learned about love from adults in your life? Do you still love your parents and family even when they make mistakes? Do you believe your parents and friends love you, even when their upset? Do you still love yourself when you make mistakes? What kind of things can make someone stop loving someone?

Affection

All types of animals show affection to show the ones they love that they love them back. For example, one of the most endearing behaviors of cats is when they head-butt you and rub against your leg. Not only is it cute to watch, but it's also a sure sign that your cat loves and cares for you. Even bigger animals such as elephants show affection. An elephant's trunk serves as its hand; the tip is, in fact, significantly more sensitive than our fingertips. Elephants stroke and caress each other's backs, and heads with their trunks to console or comfort loved ones. Elephants also make sounds to express friendliness and affection. For humans, we also use physical touch to show others that we care. Many times, we give hugs and kisses to our parents, we may pat a friend on the back, or we give friends dap or a fist pound to let them know, everything's okay. There are many types of affection, and it's important to know them and how they make you as well as others feel. Some of the most common ways our parents show us they love us and care for us are:

1) Acts of Service: People can show affection through actions such as cooking for you, cleaning for you, making something for you. Friends can show you love by helping you with homework, helping you complete an assignment at school and engaging in activities that you find pleasurable.

2) Positive Communication: People can also show you that they care by communicating with you in ways that support your growth and life. When people take the time to listen to you without judgment or motives, this is often a sign of care and love. Verbal praise and compliments are important. However, honesty, guidance and constructive critiques are also valuable in our lives and are ways that our love ones show us they love us.

3) Quality Time: People can show you they care by giving you their attention, playing games with you, helping you with homework, taking

you to practice, attending school events, sitting next to you at lunch and taking time to invest in your development as a person or professional.

4) Receiving Gifts: When people share their time, money or resources with you this can be a way of showing you they care about you. Of course, this in itself does not mean that someone loves you, however, this is often a way people choose to show their affection for people they care about.

5) Physical touch: Engaging in physical embraces such as high fives, fist pounds, hugs, kisses, and pats on the back are common ways people like to show affection. Physical touch in these manners promotes interconnection and create synchrony between people.

Critical Conversations:

Now that we know what affection can look like, let's discuss further as it's important that we know what types of affection we as well as those we care about appreciate and need. Just as we discussed before our actions communicate messages to our love ones. It's important to know and recognize what messages we are sending through our actions.

How do you show affection to people in your family? How do you and your friends show affection to each other? Who is the most affectionate person you know? If someone you have a friendship with did not show any of the types of affection listed above (Nice Words, Quality Time, Gifts, Acts of Service) would you feel that was a good friendship?

Safety Questions: Do you like the affection of others? Do you think it's ok to tell someone you trust that you don't like their type of affection? Have you ever felt uncomfortable with the affection of someone you know or didn't know?

Questions for adults: How do you show affection to the youth in your life? Do you know their preferred type of affection? How did the adults in your life show you affection? Did your early experiences with affection have an effect on how you interact with the youth in your life? Do you feel like you show your family a healthy type of affection?

Coping

Everyone needs to be able to cope with life's emotions and stresses in healthy ways. Childhood is a wonderful time to learn to cope when emotional storms come into your life. Learning how to deal with small things will build power so that if and when it is needed, you can cope and successfully handle anything life gives you. If you have excellent coping skills, you can:

- Get along better with others
- More easily make connections to others
- Be able to start and maintain friendships
- Be able to pay attention in school and learn
- Be able to handle making mistakes in sports, school or other activities
- Have more energy and tolerance for difficult life situations.
- Be more resilient as an adult

If you can imagine balancing on one leg for a long time, would it be difficult? Imagine if your goal was to balance on one leg for 10 minutes. During those 10 minutes, many things would start to affect your balance. Eventually, your leg would get tired and need some support, if you were going to continue standing on one leg. What would you do to keep your balance? You might bend your knee or put one arm out, and if needed, you would put two arms out. You do what is required in order to keep your balance.

Another example would be swimming. When you swim, you have to move your arms and legs in a synchronized motion to keep you above water and comfortable. However, what would happen if you stopped moving your arms. The answer is you would sink.

All of the things that you would do to keep from sinking in water or to stay balanced on one leg can be described as coping. Coping is when you think or behave in a way that helps keep you healthy, happy, and moving towards your goal, so you don't fall or sink into an emotional storm. If you have ever failed a test and had the thought, I'm going to study harder next time; you used coping. If you have ever played a game and loss, and you immediately started to work on the skill you needed to improve, you were coping.

Coping is like swimming; you have to actively do something to make yourself feel balanced and comfortable so you can keep moving. To stay above water, and moving in the right direction, you have to use specific movements. In life, when we go to school or at home or whenever we experience discomfort, we can sometimes get knocked off-balanced or start to sink emotionally, but just like when we were standing on one leg or when we are swimming, we have to make adjustments and COPE.

Not everyone uses positive things to cope and stay emotionally balanced. Some people choose activities that can hurt them in the future to help them handle the uncomfortable feelings they experience at that moment. Things like spending too much time on your phone, social media, video games, or friends is a form of negative coping. Some people cope by drinking alcohol or using drugs, as this helps them change the way they feel at present. The challenge with using these coping strategies is you are avoiding experiences that may be necessary and good. Just as we discussed previously this would be choosing "dirty pain". When something is difficult and knocks us off balance emotionally, we have two choices. We can choose to cope with the challenge in a clean way or we can choose to cope with the challenge in a dirty way. For example, you can cope with the news of not making the 6th grade basketball team by crying and blaming the coach, your parents and life. However, this would be selecting "dirty pain" as this will not promote the type of development needed to grow, develop and evolve into the person you want to be. It would be feeding a negative storyline that you are fragile, and life is not fair towards you specifically. The challenge with this is you are not training your mind to work through the problems life can present to you. This can lead to you avoiding work, and it can make it difficult for you to motivate yourself to do what is needed.

25

Coping is designed to support us in preventing pain; however, just like in the story, not all pain or discomfort should be avoided entirely. For example, working out can be painful. However, it should not be avoided entirely, as it is a necessary discomfort. In our previous example, a clean way to cope with not making the 6th grade basketball team would be acknowledging the disappointment and creating a practice and training schedule that allowed you to work and improve your skills. Sure, waking up early or going to bed late may be painful. However, it would be teaching and feeding a positive storyline in your brain that you are a resilient person who is willing to work for what you want. If you cope with your pain of not making the basketball team by overeating, avoiding working out, and thinking negatively, you may find yourself feeling very unhealthy physically and mentally. An important part of coping is understanding that not everything happens at the time you want it to, however, you have to "keep swimming" until it does.

What are some of the positive coping skills you have? What are some negative coping skills you have? Ask an adult about a time they had to use coping skills? Ask an adult if they are coping and working through a challenge now?

Do you know anyone who has difficulty coping with life? Do you know someone who copes well when going through an emotional storm? Who in your life has chosen dirty pain over clean pain, meaning they chose to make excuses, deny or run from the type of truth that might be healing?

Some everyday things people do to cope or fix challenges is best remembered by using the acronym COPE:

Communication: Increasing communication can help you cope by getting you more information, letting people know how you feel and helping you avoid confusion.

Answer for yourself or Ask an adult in your life how communication has helped them cope with a tough situation?

Observe: Observe means to look and notice. When you are filled with emotions because of something that happen to you, take a moment and observe and think about the situation. When you take time to think about something and look at all of the possible solutions to the problem, it can help you make better decisions that will help you not only in the present moment, but in the future as well. When emotional storms come, that can cause our vision to be blocked. Just like real storms they make it hard to see what's really going on.

For example: if you look around and see two of your friends looking in your direction and laughing. You may initially feel embarrassed or nervous. However, if you take a moment to observe the situation you could find out that there was someone behind you or something behind you that they were laughing at. Can you think of a time when you took time to look around and it helped you figure something out or problems-solve in a scary situation?

Plan, problem-solve, and participate: Planning, problem-solving, and engaging are an essential step in learning to cope. It's important to remember that in life, we can't control what happens all the time. But it is our responsibility to fix how we feel so we can reach our goal of being healthy and happy. When something happens to knock us off balance or causes us to start sinking like in a swimming pool, we have to plan out what we can do to change the situation, problem-solve the next step, and participate in bringing balance back to our lives. We have to remember we are the ones that need to take action as we are responsible for our happiness.

Have you ever solved a problem and made yourself feel better or made someone else feel better by staying calm and thinking about what you could do to fix a problem?

Exercise and controlled breathing: Going for a walk, doing something physical, or even taking time to do some mindful breathing can help you change the way your body feels. When we become upset and have an emotional storm, it can change the way our body feels. When our bodies feel angry or sad and are filled with emotion, it changes how we think and act. One way to cope or find balance is to exercise and do some mindful breathing. Taking a walk, riding your bike, or doing something physical in nature pushes negative emotions and energy out of your body. Our thoughts can tell our bodies how to feel, and when we think negative or sad thoughts, it tells our body that's the way we should be feeling, and our body tries to match it. This is hard because we often don't start feeling better until our bodies feel better. One way to get our bodies feeling better is to exercise and control our breathing.

Reciprocity

When you do something that benefits someone else, the emotional connection you've created with them makes it more likely for them to respond with a positive action that benefits you in return. This is the first type of currency humans ever had and is the most timeless form of currency we will ever use as it is universal, and everyone understands this form of payment. Reciprocity is developed and woven into good relationships, sometimes without participants knowing that is what they are doing. With awareness, it can become a natural and healthy feature of the relationship. Reciprocity requires people to be invested in their relationship. If a relationship is important enough to them, partners will be emotionally invested in it enough to work at building and maintaining it.

Success in any relationship is developed and sustained through the reward-cost balance in relationships. This means that in relationships, (mothers-son, brother-sister, husband-wife, or teacher and student) we all have to be mindful of the give and take of a relationship. If both people in the relationship are consistently giving as well as consistently accepting of love, the balance of the relationship will allow life into the relationship and the emotional cups of both people will be full.

However, a non-reciprocal love or non-reciprocal relationship can often leave you feeling drained, tired and unfulfilled. If we think of our relationship with people like a savings account at a bank. Each person has the ability to put money in as well as take money out. Using this analogy, you can imagine that if the savings account (the relationship) was going to be healthy and grow, both people would have to work as a team and consider what the other person was doing, as it would be hard to grow the account if both people were consistently taking for their own individual needs. Relationships benefit from the mutual benefits and shared interest. Reciprocity is the process of paying into the mutual interest.

Reciprocated love and emotional contribution are behavioral investments that sustain a committed relationship. To create a reciprocal relationship, both partners need to be able to accept responsibility for that creation. The interdependence of a healthy relationship requires that both people accept personal responsibility. One partner cannot take all the blame while the other partner gives all the blame. Acceptance of responsibility for the creation of a reciprocal relationship takes a high degree of emotional maturity, which takes awareness, time, and personal work to develop. This can be the most rewarding work a person will do in his or her lifetime.

Reciprocity is a great way to show people that you care and is important in keeping friendships healthy. People who are good at reciprocating are more successful, respected, and loved by their family and friends. Below are some ways to show and practice reciprocity as reciprocal relationships work in a slightly different way than it was explained in the analogy above about the savings account. This means in a relationship, not everyone will pay into the relationship in the same way. For example, in a relationship with a mother and father. A mother may work and take care of the financial parts of the home (bills, money) and the dad may stay at home and take care of the kids and the house. Both people are putting into the relationship, however, what they put in is different. This is perfectly normal and good. However, it's important to know all the different ways people can add value to relationships so that you can appreciate all forms of reciprocity. If we only accept money or certain forms of reciprocity, we may be tricked by others as we may feel that they care for us just by the types of reciprocating they show us. Below are the most common forms of reciprocity we receive from our family and friends.

Time: Helping a parent cook, watching a show with someone, accompanying someone on an outing, talking with someone. When you spend time with someone, you are showing them you like their company and enjoy being around them. Many people value this form of reciprocity and this is how they prefer people pay into relationships with them.

Energy: When you help someone with a project or give your energy to something that is not just for you, it makes people feel you care for them and are invested in their success and happiness. Many people value the energy and life others bring to relationships. This is often the form of reciprocity children show to their grandparents and parents. Children have energy and life due to their youth and age. Adults and the elderly value and appreciate the energy and life the youth bring.

Can you think of ways you bring energy and life to the people in your life?

Resources: When you share with someone, you are showing them that you care about them in the same manner that you care about yourself. You are being selfless, which means you are connecting with them on an emotional level. Not everyone has a lot of money, however, there are a lot of ways to share what you have. When you give, even when you don't have a lot, it really shows others you care.

Have you ever given or has someone ever given to you even when they didn't have to? How do you feel when people share their resources with you?

Questions for youth: Which one of the forms of showing reciprocity do you use? Which one do you like when people use with you? Do your parents have a form of reciprocating that makes you feel good? Do you think they like the way you show them reciprocity or give back to them? How do you add to the life of your friends? How do they add to your life? Which form of reciprocity is more difficult for you? Think about the relationships you have, are there healthy forms are reciprocity being displayed? Describe a relationship you have and why it is reciprocal? Describe a relationship you have, or you've seen that lacks reciprocity?

Takeaway Skills:

Our emotions stem from our relationships, and these emotions develop at an early age based on our experiences. They can affect how we feel about ourselves and how we grow as people as our experiences

31

live in our minds as well as our bodies and nervous systems. This means our behavior and mental health is affected by how our minds as well as bodies feel. For example, a cardiologist (a doctor who takes care of people's hearts) is just as likely to overeat and develop the same vulnerability to heart disease as anyone else. Some might think that as a heart doctor, they would know what to do in order to have a healthy heart. However, knowing something is not the only thing required to do something. We must consider that our bodies and nervous systems also affect our behavior and decisions. Knowing how to listen to our minds as well as bodies is important, and we have to create environments that allow us to talk about how we as well as others feel. Perceiving a lack of love, affection, and that you don't have the ability to cope can cause us to develop poor thinking habits and coping skills that can make it difficult to change even when we know it would be in our best interest to do so.

The focus of this chapter is about creating a strong foundation for understanding emotions and how we have to develop a healthy emotions root system. The key elements of this stage of development are Trust vs. Mistrust. When developing strong and healthy relationships with our families, it provides us with a sense of "HOPE" that we carry into our interactions with the rest of the world.

Further, this structures our brain in a way that teaches us to look for the positive in a situation as opposed to looking for the problem. The thing to remember is that healthy relationships can shape our brain's structure and functioning. Likewise, so does unhealthy relationships

Chapter 2

Learning the Ways of the Weather

As time went by the parents were appreciating their little seed. They
were doing all they could to help her succeed.

They read stories, they went to soccer games, and they even planned for
college with money pledged in her name.

However, in life, seasons do change
and we have to adjust when things rearrange.

On the seed's birthday it seems something was on the verge and sure
enough, there was a trunk beginning to emerge.

The parent's little child was no longer a seed,
it had grown into a young tree, a young tree indeed.

With the emergence of this trunk a personality grew, and the little seed
was not so little as it began to have an opinion too.

As the trunk broke through the ground, that's when things became a
mess, the tree was now more affected by the weather, and even started to
feel stress.

Stress is when you don't feel balance and it's hard to recover, stress is
what it feels like if you are at a big park and you lose sight of your
mother.

You feel upset in your body and your mind, and when you look for
peace, it's hard for you to find.

When stress takes over, it makes you think of only one thought,
and you can't think of all the wonderful things you were taught.

In the case of little tree, her thinking was fast, and it felt like she had put on an emotional mask.

The little tree was experiencing emotions,
and now that she lived above ground, she experienced life outside of her parent's devotion.

So when things happen that would make the little tree mad, the parents were at a loss, as they did not share all the experiences the little tree had.

On one day in particular, there was a small storm, and the little tree woke up under it, so she took the same form.

She felt cold and unloved and wanted to be left alone.
When her parents said good morning she took an angry tone.

She said, "Leave me alone and just get out of my way."

Her parents said, "
Excuse me young tree that is not a nice thing to say."

The tree started crying and went into a rage, the parents were alarmed as this was not typically how their little tree behaved.

Their little tree had an emotional storm that they were starting to feel, and the parents were getting upset as with their own emotions they had to deal.

The parents were now angry, and it was not hard to tell, as mom was screaming, and dad was pale.

The parent's emotions were creating a negative wind, and before you knew it the little trees trunk was starting to bend.

When the parents notice their creation, they decided to retreat, to remove the negative sensations.

Just as the parents recovered from the tension, they remember what the big beautiful tree had mentioned;
"Happiness is the sun, learning is the rain. Darkness is inevitable so teach skills to work through the pain."

As the mom saw her baby tree acting in defiance, she ran to the forest looking for more guidance.

The big beautiful tree said,
"I know why you're here; the trunk of your tree is starting to appear.

The trunk of the tree is starting to show, and this is important as it will filter what comes up from the roots below.

The only problem is the trunk is very fragile and it wants what it wants so you have to prepare it for battle."

"The parents said, "Okay, great, so what do we do?"
The big beautiful tree said, "I'll walk you through..."

We have to build the bark even if it feels like madness
as this will protect the trunk from the weather
as the weather can carry sadness."

"The bark is toughness it protects the trunk of your tree,
so the winds carrying negative emotions (anger, fear, jealousy)
will just let it be.

Teach your tree the ways of the weather,
in order to do this you have to be clever.

It's tricky to know, the weather pattern you see, because the weather we
feel can come from you and from me.

When we feel emotions, we create our own storms and if others are
around us they may take the same form.

Our trunks have two roles, to protect and to school,
so when we experience bad weather, we block it and use our tools to
remain calm and cool.

An exposed trunk with no bark is vulnerable you see, as elements from
outside will tear away at the poor tree.

Darkness builds bark but only for a limited time; if it stays dark for too
long that's not a good sign."

The parents accepted the knowledge and they ran on to finish their day.
They had a new outlook and vowed to change their way

In the days to come, the parents wanted to help little tree build tools,
they figured it would be important as the tree was starting school.

The young tree went to school with the trunk on full display, but just as recess hit a kid on the playground didn't feel in the best way.

The boy yelled and screamed obscenities
and then walked away.
This was certainly not how little tree wanted to spend her day.

The boy had created an emotional storm, and little tree was the recipient,
so she took the same form.

The boy at school had sent a storm of madness and directly following
behind was wind carrying sadness.

Little tree became of those emotions as she was in his storm.

When the tree made it home
they knew their little tree was not in the best form.

The parents were aware, that a storm had come, they decided to talk to find out the damage that had been done.

The parents saw darkness, but they knew it could build bark.
So, they intervened,
so the wind from the storm would not leave a mark.

They explained the Wind, and why it came, they said the boy was obviously in a lot of pain,
they told their little tree to learn from the wind and when it happens again to use its bark as toughness to defend.

The little tree asked a great big question, she said, "What is bark as I haven't learned that lesson?"

The parents said,
"The bark is your thoughts and how they can make you feel, when you have positive thoughts, the weather sits still.

We have to see the world in a positive way and make rules for our thoughts so the good ones will stay.

Rule number one is likely the best lesson, as it is loving yourself defends against depression.

Rule number two is equally as brilliant, as it requires that you know in life you have to be resilient.

Resilience is when you believe you can recover, and when one thing doesn't work, you are brave enough to try another.

Rule number three is one for health, as this is one where you have to check in on yourself.

Taking time daily to think about you, will help you filter your negative emotions and just let them pass through.

When you check on yourself,
you can learn what creates your own bad weather,
so instead of getting upset you can just be clever."

When it was all said and done the tree had gained new bark and the next day at school she showed up with no marks.

The parents reflected and thought about the day, they realized the darkness is inevitable but should not go completely away.

They thought their tree needed darkness, to use it and learn,
if little tree was afraid of darkness,
she would always be worried or concerned.

Running from hard times will not help you grow, as it is the hard times that makes roots stronger below.

When you can learn from hard times it can help you succeed because hard times build toughness and toughness is what we need.

Goals and Guidelines for age 9 through 12:

Recognize and manage emotions and behavior.

1. Describe the body's physical responses to common emotions such as anger, sadness, grief, anxiety.
2. Discuss how experiences from people you love or consider important have negatively affected your thoughts and self-talk or positively affected your self-talk.
3. Identify and discuss experiences that are or were difficult that may have occurred due to your race, culture, religion, gender or personal beliefs.
4. Practice expressing gratitude and positive feelings about others.
5. Explain the importance of responding to upsetting or troubling times as oppose to reacting.

Develop understanding of the emotional skills related to relationships.

1. Describe how peoples feeling can change about the same topic depending on circumstances.
2. Describe a disagreement you had with another person and summarize both points of view.
3. Evaluate how changing your behavior affects the behavior of others.

Teaching Points and Critical Conversations

Positive self-talk:

People who learn to manage their emotions have healthy self-talk. Self-talk is the little voice you use to explain things to yourself. It's regularly communicating with you to help you interpret and understand things and to prepare you for new ideas. You can think of the thoughts like a DJ on the radio or at a school dance, but only this DJ lives in your head. It's part of you, and you can never leave them behind. Also, this DJ has songs, music, images, movie clips, snippets from your life, and internet storylines picked from our culture that can be used to create an atmosphere or storyline in your head. This can be a positive thing or a negative thing depending on the story being created by you. As we go through our day this can be background music or it can take center stage and create an internal world that is so influential you feel that everyone can see and hear the story in your head, further this atmosphere can drive you to act with 100 percent intensity as your internal DJ has set the mood so well, but reality may not match what is going on inside your head.

Example #1:

Setting the scene: If you have negative self-talk related to your ability as a soccer player and you are attending a tryout for a new team. The DJ in your head may bring up clips of you missing a goal, people making faces of disapproval and telling people you messed-up. You start thinking and telling yourself that things are not going to go well, because you are not really that good of a soccer player. You start to feel nervous in your mind and body, your legs start to feel weaker than normal and you start to think soccer is just not for you. (The internal DJ has created a story for you).

Reality: The tryout begins with a scrimmage and you are so nervous and weak in the legs you are allowing people who are typically not as fast as you run by you because your legs are weak from your nerves, you miss an opportunity to kick a goal because you are a step behind everyone else, due to your negative thinking.

Response: You say in your mind, "I knew I didn't deserve to be here, I'm not as good as these kids and these last two plays prove it. Everyone must think I really suck and I'm not as good as they once thought I was in the past."

Explanation: Your mind and body are responding to the story you created in your head. Your body can't tell the difference between reality and the reality you have created in your mind. In fact, the story you create in your mind is much more powerful than reality. The truth in this example could be that you were invited to the tryout because you are worthy of being there. Everyone else on the field is just as nervous and if you played to the level your capabilities, you would do great. When you are nervous and thinking too much, it is typical that your performance decreases so if you stop thinking about negative things and just stay in the moment, you would be just fine.

Example #2:

Setting the scene: Example: Having negative self-talk related to your mom, as you might think she is mean or doesn't love you unless you earn all A's on your report card. In this situation the DJ in your head will bring up clips of her raising her voice at you or making faces of disapproval and telling you that you don't try hard enough. You keep telling yourself that if she feels this way that maybe you should treat her mean or give up. You start to feel angry in your mind and body, your eyes puff up, and you begin to think she only cares about your grades. (The internal DJ has set the environment in your head).

Interaction with reality: Your mom comes by and asks you how you are doing in school.

Response: You become emotional and say something that hurts her feelings.

Explanation: You have just responded to the story the DJ in your head created, it is in your mind. You did not respond to reality and what was really going on. This prevents you from responding in a way that would lead to more positive results. The truth was your mom was checking in about school; however, the thoughts in your head lead you to think something different. This is why having positive self-talk is so important.

Family Discussion Questions: Do you have positive self-talk? When does yourself talk become negative? Is it when you make a mistake? Do you have positive self-talk in some areas of your life and negative self-talk in other areas of your life?

Questions for adults in your life: Do you believe your negative self-talk comes from the negative experiences in your life? Do you think the self-talk of the youth in your life comes from their interactions with you and other adults? What affect do your interactions with the child in your life have on their self-talk and inner life?

Building Bark or Toughness:

Toughness comes from what you know, what you want, and what you do. There will always be people in life or situations that are not simple and can be hard to handle. These situations can make it tough for you to COPE or stay balanced. However, building bark or being mentally tough is when you have a protective mental barrier around you so that the storms created by other people don't move you or the storms created by life don't shake you. Toughness comes from three things 1) what you know, 2) what you want, and 3) what you do.

What you Know:

We know that our emotions are a natural part of life, but we cannot allow them to run our life. We have to practice removing emotions and our personal story from the events that happen (objectivity). We have to guard against the wind of emotion knocking us off our feet. Let's take some situations that have happened to many people and use them as an example.

Situation 1: You receive an (F) on a test, and your parents are furious, and they take away your phone privileges.

Situation 2: Your former best friend is bullying you at school as she has become friends with a group of people who don't like you.

Situation 3: You've been cut from the volleyball team after playing for five years with your friends, and now you are the only one of your friends that did not make the team.

These are all events and things that can happen. However, until we add our personal feelings to the circumstances, they remain circumstantial events. One way to practice mental toughness is WHAT YOU KNOW. You have to know the trick of seeing what helps you succeed in every situation. All of these situations mean nothing until you add your own thoughts and meaning to it. When you add in how you think you are supposed to feel or you simply accept the feelings that come to you from the event, you are giving the event power over you. When we see obstacles or things that happen, we have a choice. We can say, "I received an F on a test, and my parents are mad, which would be the facts. The second part we have control over. We can either tell our self this is bad; I'm a failure and fall into emotions that lead to more negative thoughts and habits. Or we can say, "I received an F on a test," which are the facts and let our feelings and emotions pass through like clouds and determine how we will respond to the situation. We don't have to be a victim of our feelings and the negative thoughts they carry with them. So often, through movies, tv, books, media, and even the adults in our life, we learn that we have to label the events that happen to us, and we often know the expected emotions we should feel when it happens. For example, if you receive an (F) on a test, you should feel ashamed, or if your friends are saying mean things to you, you should be sad and hurt, or if you get cut from the volleyball team, you should be embarrassed. However, it's vital to practice objectivity and action. Objectivity means seeing only the facts about something that happen and leaving your personal story or beliefs about what that means out of it as it's not needed and will not help you at the time. ACTION means looking and searching for a solution to the obstacle and working to achieve success.

Many successful people have taken this approach and used it to improve their life. For example, let's take Michael Jordan, arguably one of the greatest basketball players to ever play in the NBA. Michael Jordan was cut from his 9th-grade basketball team as the coach did not think he was talented enough. Those were the facts. However, Michael did not add his emotional story and meaning to the event. He did not get stuck on the fact that his parents might be disappointed or that he must be a failure. Instead, Michael Jordan chose to accept the reality of the situation and take action. His action was that he was going to wake up early and outwork every player on the team so he could change the fact that he did not make the team.

45

Mental toughness comes from the KNOWING that nothing can hurt you unless you give it permission and power through the meaning you give to it. If you don't provide it with authority and power, it cannot hurt you know matter what. Let's take another example. Harriet Tubman was a woman of small stature who was born into slavery. This meant she was born into a situation where the reality meant that she was the property of another human being. If she attempted to free herself or her family, she would be killed or significantly harmed. Harriet could have added her own emotional story to this and added her own emotional meaning. However, like emotions often do, it would have left her stuck, scared, and prevented her from ACTION. Thankfully Harriet Tubman chose to see only the facts and then take the action that was needed to change her situation and the situation of over 300 slaves. Harriet learned and studied the area in which she lived and found a secret passageway out that led her to freedom. However, instead of just saving herself, Harriet made dozens of trips back into the slave riddled south to save others. She accomplished this because she chose to see what would help her succeed. So, the next time something happens in your life that feels like an emotional storm, remember, you don't have to let emotions rule the day and stop you from acting heroically. You can choose to allow the feelings and the negative thoughts that they bring to pass through you and then take action to your goal. Think of Michael Jordan, Harriet Tubman, and the many everyday heroes that we don't have the pleasure of knowing who overcame challenges that many people think are insurmountable. However, they beat these challenges because they SEE WHAT HELPS THEM SUCCEED. It's important to note that emotions are not bad, rather they are one of many ways we receive messages. However, emotions are not meant to be the final decision-makers, and we often allow them to stay too long and make more decisions than they should. Every day we have to practice putting emotions in their place, and we need to know how to allow feelings and emotions to pass through so we can take action.

Below are daily steps that you can practice that will help you build your mental muscle so you can push emotions out when big emotional storms come through.

Allowing emotions to pass through is as simple as A, B, C!

Affirmations: Affirmations are positive statements that can help you to challenge and overcome doubt, negative thoughts, and the feelings that come along with those thoughts. When you repeat them often and believe in them, you can start to make positive changes. Many of us do repetitive exercises to improve our physical health, and affirmations are like exercises for our mind and outlook. These positive mental repetitions can reprogram our thinking patterns so that, over time, we begin to think – and act – differently, and the positive thoughts become our automatic thoughts. Some research shows that about 95% of our automatic thoughts are negative. They are often things we have heard from people in our lives and media. We have to actively work and practice every day to change these automatic thoughts so that when we experience a situation, we can start to say our affirmations and change the way our body feels.

Breath: Intentional deep breathing improves mental health by relaxing both the body and the mind. When we take slow, deep breaths, we increase oxygen in our bloodstream and thus in our brain. Deep breathing signals the parasympathetic nervous system to activate and thus induce relaxation throughout the body. When we pause to breathe deeply, our heart rate slows, and our blood pressure decreases. All of this positive activity increases our wellbeing.

We lose our sense of stress when our body relaxes as we breathe deeply. We feel fewer negative emotions, and our mind becomes quieter our thoughts stiller. Deep breathing reduces feelings of stress, anxiety, and calms people's frustrations. While deep breathing doesn't cure mental illness, it calms people and in so doing, increases positive mental health.

Practice working on your breathing should be done every day as it is like a muscle, and the more you practice, the better you get. When you practice breathing, it makes it more likely that you can control your breathing when emotion passes through you. Breathing is the most critical thing you can do to help your emotions pass on through.

Commit: Committing to the belief that you look for what helps you succeed. Commit to knowing that there are no good things that happen in life or bad things, just events, and situations you have to label. We have to add meaning to the events in our life. We also have to commit to knowing that work, persistence, and perseverance are part of life and should be part of our success. If your definition of success or happiness does not include perseverance and determination, it means that you will be stopped at the first obstacles you see.

True success in life, school, relationships, and in our career comes from overcoming obstacles as nothing worth having comes without obstacles. You have to commit to knowing that there will always be people, even people who love you, that will sometimes put an emotional spin on something that happens. Although they have good intentions, they may attempt to bring you under the emotional storm with them. When this happens, you have to commit to seeing the solution for success and taking action needed to be successful in the situation.

Who is the most mentally tough person, you know? Are you able to overcome big emotions to solve problems or do what's needed?

What we want:

Top-level athletes and achievers in all fields all set goals. Setting goals gives you an idea of what you will be in the future and motivation to try to achieve that future in the present moment. It gives you a focus point, just like when we discussed standing on one leg trying to keep your balance, setting goals each and every day gives you the same type of focus and balance. It also helps us focus on what we want to learn, and helps you to organize your time so that you can make the most of your day.

By setting sharp, clear goals, you can measure and take pride in the achievement of those goals, and you'll see progress and not just the boredom of doing something repeatedly. You will also raise your self-confidence, as you will be proving to yourself what you can do.

Ask an Adult or a Friend if they set daily or weekly goals? How do goals help them focus? How do goals help balance their emotions?

What you do: Action is an important ingredient to building toughness for two reasons; first, it's what you do to prove to yourself who you are and who you want to be. Second, it is part of the toughness process that affects the world. It's important to behave in ways that confirm who you are and who you want to be. This does not mean you have to be perfect every day, but it means that you should have personal goals every day. When you meet your personal goals, you are building a belief in yourself and strengthening your thoughts. As you continue to develop these beliefs, you will become stronger and closer to the best version of yourself. For example, if you play a sport at recess or an instrument in a band or even reading in class and you are not very good at this time. If people make fun of you or you feel shame, that can be hard. However, if you are proving to yourself every day that you are working on getting better, and you are setting small goals, you are building and strengthening your belief so that comments and negative people no longer bother you.

This can be aided by developing Healthy habits. Healthy habits can make it easier for you to be mentally tough because you train yourself to do what is needed. Building healthy habits can increase mental toughness because you will be a stronger and more prepared person. For example, if you have a habit of getting enough sleep, you will be better able to focus in class. If you have a habit of eating healthy foods, you will have energy throughout the day. If you have a habit of doing homework, you will be more prepared in class. When you have a habit of speaking and being kind to people, people will want to return your kindness. Habits are things that you do every day that become part of who you are.

Do you have healthy sleeping, eating, and studying habits? Do you have a habit of doing something every day that will make you better at a goal? How much time do you spend on task that are not related to your goals?

Mental toughness toolkit

When you act proactively, it keeps you mentally tough because you can sometimes avoid unfortunate situations or make them easier to handle. Behaviors that support mental toughness include:

Being assertive: Showing confidence and stating how you feel or what you need. Being assertive is putting the world on notice that you know who you are, and you have boundaries that you will protect. Think of this as a car horn. Have you ever been in a car with an adult, and they had to blow their horns to get other driver's attention? There are many ways to blow your horn that communicates different messages to people. A quick hit of the horn serves as a reminder or alert. A long and extended press of the horn can seem more aggressive and can cause a lot of emotions in the person who you're directing it at. Being assertive should be like a quick hit of the horn. It's your way of letting others know you are there, and they have to be aware of your presence, but it should not be aggressive.

Ask an adult about a time where they had to honk their horn or be assertive? Have you ever had to honk your horn or be assertive to get what you want or need?

Problem solving: A problem solver is someone who always believes there is a way to solve a problem that works out for their best interest or that teaches you a lesson. Problem solvers can find a positive in any situation. Sometimes we can train our minds to attach and hold on to negative things. For example, if you receive some upsetting news about

50

not being able to attend a field trip because you didn't turn in your permission slip. A problem solver will think of ways to either overcome the challenge or if the challenge can't be changed, they think of ways they can think about the problem that makes them feel better. For example, a problem solver may think that they will return their permission slip early the next time so they can ensure a spot on the bus.

Seeking help: We all benefit from seeking the advice and guidance from someone who can see beyond our current situation. If you have ever stared at a picture for a long time, the picture may start to get blurry and you can easily miss something in front of you. This is what can happen to us when we have different challenges or situations in our life. We sometimes are so close to the events in our life that we can't see things clearly. Having a trusted person to help you bring things back in focus is important.

Critical Conversations:

Have you ever had to use one of the mental toughness action skills? Which one is the easiest for you? Which skill is most difficult for you? Are these skills harder to use with different people? How does Prayer/Meditation/Mindfulness/time away help you with your emotions? What are some experiences that helped you build bark or made you tougher and stronger? What songs, quotes, or stories does your internal DJ bring to your mind when you are feeling mentally tough? e.g

Authors note:

Our emotions can be affected by our own thoughts or the behavior and emotions of others. Regardless of who brought the big emotions to us, whether it is another person or from our own thoughts, it is our own responsibility to think and act in a way the restores our balance. This is an important social emotional standard to teach our children. This means we are the ones that have to be resilient and work through our emotions so we can continue on with our day and meet our goals. Understanding that emotions are like the weather can help our children grow as when they experience emotions they know that it does not determine their life, rather it's something that will pass through and they should not make really big decisions based on something that will not last long. This also supports children in learning about the refractory period which is the period of time it takes them to recover from emotional events. When our children /youth, gain this understanding they will be able to develop an understanding of how emotions feel and how to help them past through.

Takeaway skills: Have you ever noticed that you were in a bad mood and you wanted to get out of it, but you just couldn't shake it off? Or have you ever had a mound of homework but realized you're not in the mood to get it done? Sometimes we can be a prisoner of our mood and a hostage to the moment, but we don't have to be as moods aren't things that just happen to us. We can affect and change them.

Being able to choose the mood that's best suited to a situation is one of the skills of emotional intelligence. Choosing the right mood can help you control whatever situation you're in and help you live a long and healthy life. Think of your mood like a puppeteer who has strings on your arms and legs. Moods have the power to make you think and act in the way it wants you to.

Moods can influence how well we do in certain situations but they are not something we should trust as they can change just like the seasons. However, our mindset is something that can also affect our thoughts and behaviors, and it is under our control.

What's the difference between a mood and a mindset? Moods are the emotions we feel. A mindset is the thoughts and ideas that go along with that mood. Mood and mindset go hand in hand because our thoughts can influence our mood.

Here's an example: Imagine you're competing in a swim meet this afternoon. Which mood and mindset helps you do your best?

Mood A: **Insecure**. You keep thinking about how the other swimmers might blow you out of the water and maybe you're not good enough to be on the team.

Mood B: **Annoyed**. You're thinking about how swimming interferes with your social life. You tell yourself you're missing out on so many other things.

Mood C: **Pumped up and confident.** You're thinking that if you do your best, there's a good chance your team can place well.

Of course, you're likely to do your best with the mood and mindset in option C. But what if you're feeling A or B and worry that those moods might affect your performance? Luckily, you can change your mood.

How to Choose a Mood

Step 1: Identify your mood. To switch moods, listen to your thoughts and feelings. That way you can decide if you need to change your mood to one that matches your situation. Think about or write down the type of thoughts that go with the mood you want to be in.

To identify a mood, stop and think about what you're feeling and why. Put those feelings into words, like, "Wow, I'm really sad right now" or "I'm feeling really alone." You can say this silently to yourself, out loud, or to someone else.

Step 2: Accept what you feel. After you name your emotion, show yourself some understanding for feeling the way you do. It's perfectly OK (and natural!) to feel bored on a rainy Saturday, annoyed about having to study when everyone else is going out or angry if you have been in the car with your brother or sister for three hours. All emotions are acceptable and understandable. But you don't have to hold on to feeling that way. Notice your mood, then choose to move past it.

Step 3: Pick the mood that's best for the situation you are in. If you're competing in a swim meet, it's best to be pumped up and confident. If you need to get down to some serious studying, it's better to feel interested, alert, and confident (and not so helpful to feel grumpy, annoyed, and self-defeated). Take a minute to think about which emotions will help you accomplish your goal.

How to Get Into the Best Mood

After you imagine the mood that works best for your task or situation, it's time to get into that mood. Think "P for positive" and focus on these 6 things that can help you reset your mood:

Purpose. Get clear on what you want and need to do. For example, you might want to get your homework done so you can go on an outing with your parents. In this case it would be important to set your intentions.

Place. Ask your parents or an adult if you need permission to put yourself in the right situation or environment. Being in a comfortable environment influences mood. If you need to calm down, it's better to find a quiet space, instead of staying in the same place that made you upset.

Positive People. Who can help you feel the way you need to feel? A focused classmate is a better study companion than a chatty friend. Sometimes, just thinking of a particular person is enough to help you feel confident, inspired, strong, or supported.

Playlist. Music is one of the most powerful influences on mood because it's all about communicating and inspiring emotion. Create playlists for the moods that are the most helpful and positive for your life.

Posture. Move your body into the right mood. Try exercises that help you focus on your physical posture like yoga or t'ai chi. For energy, try a workout that gets your heart rate up. To prepare for sleep, try deep breathing, gentle stretching, or other soothing activities.

Positive Promotion. Encourage yourself with self-talk. Self-talk is a way of using thoughts to influence your mood. If you've ever said to yourself, "OK, let's get serious for a minute" or "I can do this!" you've used self-talk to get into the right mood for a situation. Self-talk doesn't just create the mindset that supports your mood; it also helps you keep a mood going. That's why pep talks work so well for athletes.

How to Get Out of an Unhelpful Mood

To get out of a mood that's unpleasant or unhelpful, think "U for U-turn." Try these mood changers:

Undo. Break the leash. Negative thoughts are like a leash that keeps you stuck and brings you back to the negative thoughts you were thinking. It's very powerful and you have to have a strong desire to break the leash. Your desire to break the leash has to be stronger than your negative thoughts and emotions. Ways to break through the leash are to engage in mindfulness activities. Mindfulness means that you stay in the present moment and enjoy being present in your environment. This is where the analogy "stop and smell the roses" comes from. It means, take time to appreciate where you are and what you are doing. Many times, when we are feeling negative it's because we are thinking about the future or thinking about the past. Negative thoughts about the future is the definition of anxiety. When you consciously take 10 minutes to notice 5 things in your environment, 4 sensations you are currently feeling in your body, 3 things that you can hear, 2 things that you smell and 1 image that comes to your mind, you are engaging with your present reality.

Unstick. When you recognize that you are in a negative mood, picture yourself on a dog leash or as if you have just been bit by a spider that has venom that leaves you motionless. The point is, visualizing how your mood can affect your behavior is important. Remember bad moods and poor thinking is like a dog leash as it can keep you from moving beyond the way you currently feel. Just like the spider bite example negative moods have the ability to keep you still, prevent new and refreshing thoughts and prevent you from taking action until the venom is gone. In order to break the leash or shake off the effects of the venom you must physically change your body posture or engage in action that can change your body chemistry. Things like exercising, striking a power pose, or smiling in the mirror can do wonders for changing your mood. The point is you have to train yourself to think better than you feel. This can be hard as our emotions can be convincing as they cause physical sensations. However, emotions are not always truthful and should not always be the final decision maker.

Unwind. Imagine yourself fishing and you hook a fish. When you hook the fish, you have to reel it in. Think of the calm mood like the fish you are going to reel in slowly. The fish is going to want to go back into the water, but you just keep reeling the fish in and eventually you will have it. Ways to reel in that calm mood are: sit quietly, breathe gently, and focus on each breath. To keep your mind from wandering back to a mood you're trying to change, every time you take a breath, think about the fish slowly coming back towards the bank every time you breathe deeply.

It's important to remember that you've probably chosen your mood before without even realizing it. Many times people choose a mood naturally without thinking about it. But practicing ways to choose your mood intentionally can help you get good at it.

So next time you feel a strong mood, stop and name it. Ask yourself if it's the best mood for what you're trying to accomplish. Sometimes, even the happiest of moods might not be right for a particular situation (as anyone who's excited about weekend plans during Friday afternoon classes knows).

How parents can help:

Parents can help their children/youth name it to tame it! This means you can point out in a non-aggravating way when you notice your child/youth in a mood or under the influence of an emotional storm. One way to do this is to connect be for you direct. What this means is if you notice your child or youth in a mood that may be keeping them stuck, think about connecting with them on an emotional level first as they will likely be using only the emotional aspects of their brain. Once you have connected, you can remind them that they have a choice and they can choose to keep this current mood or break the chains and pick a mood that better fits the situation. For example, if you see your son or daughter becoming frustrated over every little thing that happens, you may want to tell them quickly to change their mood as they have nothing to be irritated about. However, the truth is they are irritated, and they also feel irritated. Connecting before directing would be empathizing and pointing out that you notice and see the variables in their life that can cause them to feel upset. Once you have validated how they feel and become an emotional ally, you can give direction that will support them in changing how they feel.

Chapter 3

Big and Beautiful Like Me

One day in the spring, the parents looked around;
they saw all the flowers with beautiful colors
that illuminated the ground.

Their hearts were so pleasant as they looked at their
young tree, they smiled in
amazement at how polite she had grown to be.

With the passing of spring, things started to change, as the young
tree had new urgings that occupied her brain.

The day she turned13, she had strong motivation;
she wanted to leave childhood behind and find friends with a
more adult orientation.

In order to do this,
she thought a couple of things must be understood, the first thing
she needed to do was to part with childhood.

When she thought of how to do this, what popped in her mind,
was to break up with her parents,
as this was a childhood sign.

No more cuddling, niceties, or childish games, they had to know I
was growing, and things wouldn't be the same.

With this new pressure to grow, it made life quite hard,
as she didn't depend on her parents as she would rather starve.

One day things would be great and the next,
it would be a mess. She could hardly figure out how to handle all
of the stress.

She would make a good decision
and at times it would feel bad. The tree would wonder how
positive choices could make you feel sad.

Still at other times bad decisions she would make,
and she felt like they were coming in every aspect of her life.
This she could not take.

The young tree felt as if she had no way to deal and this would
sometimes cause her just to sit still.

She would stay in her room and go into deep thought, but she noticed the thoughts didn't match what she was taught.

She was thinking poorly, and about negative things and sometimes wondered if she would ever experience the joy of spring.

Well, in little tree's defense it had grown to be a hectic time, no one had noticed all the warning signs.

The warning signs were clear, they were all in the same section. What the parents didn't notice was all the branches growing in multiple directions.

Soccer was a branch; school was one too even social life had a branch, so dad wanted one too.

The parents were worried, with the appropriate terror, if the tree stayed under this much pressure, there was bound to be an unfortunate error. The parents were quick and rushed to the forest as the big beautiful tree would surely have advice for us.

The big beautiful tree said, "I know why you're here, it's because your young trees path is not very clear. I can also provide another guess to match this, as I predict your tree has started to grow branches."

This is an important time and I'm glad you decided to show. What you see in the middle of the trunk Are branches and they carry the weight of all the beautiful things that your tree has the potential to grow.

Each branch of your tree is fed and maintained by the stem, and if
the tree is going to be successful it has to know how much energy
to give to them.

This challenge and responsibility are necessary you see, as growth
only comes from a gradual increase in responsibility.

The parents were still confused,
but yet, they knew the tree was not wrong.
So, they ask,
"How do we keep our young tree's stem strong?"

It is important in this stage that trees learn to work together as having good influences can protect you from bad weather.

Friends are important, but they shouldn't be your entire locus as
this concentration will make you lose focus.

At this stage for a tree, the tree needs balance as too many things
going on will diffuse its talents.

Setting small goals each and every day will help your young tree
and serve as a path to guide her way.

The parents of the tree were excited, yet nervous as this was a time
where they could provide a different type of service.

In the days to come, it was amazing to see as they taught the
young tree to approach the world with a renewed energy.

She was balanced in her mind, and saw through emotional storms,
she even felt compassion for people who tried to get her to change
her form.

With this new approach to life, spring was always here,
she now lived her life without terror and fear.

Her confidence was high because she monitored her thoughts and
if they went awry, you know they would be caught.

With practice she worked to manage her mind, and this helped
her grow to be beautiful and divine.

At the end of this period the parents started to see,
after all these stages, they had finally
developed a beautiful tree.

When the tree was fully grown, she made a visit you see, as it was
only right, she went to see the big beautiful tree.

The tree said,
"I know why you are here, you don't have to tell me, as it is time
to take your place in the world and be proud and free."

Chapter 4
Teaching Points and Critical Conversations

Science of Adolescents:

Daniel Siegel, PhD, talks about the E.S.S.E.N.C.E. of adolescence in his book, *Brainstorm: The Power and Purpose of the Teenage Brain*. He describes how the ESSENCE of the teenage mind presents wonderful opportunities and frightening risks for parents and teens. If a parent tries to stifle, muzzle, or oppose this ESSENCE, the teen may rebel, withdraw, or even experience a decrease in motivation. Instead, parents do well to engage their teen's ESSENCE and creatively collaborate with their teen to help them harness, guide, and find healthy expressions for it.

If we can understand our children's innate goals, we can support them in reaching their destination. In addition to knowing the goals of our children, we have to know what biologically they will be contending with. We have to know the ESSENCE of adolescence. ESSENCE is an acronym that represents four aspects of the teenager's changing brain (coined by Dr, Daniel Siegel and Tina Payne Bryson).

E.S. - Emotional Spark. The reward circuits in a teenager's brain are undergoing major remodeling. This is for good reason as they are preparing for a time where they will experience the world without adult leadership and guidance. Inevitably this transition will come with its up's and downs. During adolescence, the reward circuit's exhibit increased activity that result in teens feeling bored with everyday life while gravitating toward thrilling and exhilarating experiences. In addition, teens are experiencing epic changes in their bodies, relationships, and their role in their family. Change is uncomfortable for everyone, so for teens, emotions such as moodiness, impulsiveness, and reactivity are part of the experience as the intensity of change is occurring on multiple levels. On the positive side, these changes fill you with a zest for life and a drive to do something new and exciting in the world. Many of the greatest inventions and technology we have today come from the minds of adolescents. As parents we can nourish and cultivate that emotional spark and help them focus that energy on goals and aspirations. You can support your teen through teaching them how to regulate their mind and body. Emotional energy is never lost and can only change forms. If you don't properly know how to manage and or release emotional energy it can and often does become stuck in your mind or body. This is called a somatic symptom. A somatic symptom is a physical sensation or pain that originated as a psychological challenge. For example, if a person experiences an upset stomach that was caused by intense worry or anxiety. This can be a great source of struggle for teens and adults alike as many of us don't have healthy routines that help us use and release emotional energy. It's important that we pay close attention to our sleeping, eating, water drinking and exercise habits. The above-mentioned activities are easily and often overlooked as they can seem simple. However, the truth is that most teens and adults don't receive the proper nutrition, don't receive enough sleep, are chronically dehydrated and don't engage in an appropriate exercise routine. These respective activities are key in appropriately managing emotions and being empowered by the natural emotional spark we have as teens.

How do you handle big emotions? How often do you experience emotions that change the way you feel and think? In what situations or environments are your emotions the strongest? In what environment are you most at piece? In what environment are you most stressed?

What's something in life that you are passionate about? Do you feel you often have lots of energy and emotion? Or, too little energy and emotion?

S.E.- Social Engagement. Teens exhibit an increased desire for peer relationships. Peers become a driving force in teenagers' lives. Peer relationships provide mutual support in navigating the multiple changes teens experience in their life. In fact, research suggests positive peer relationships during the teen years are the best predictor of well-being, longevity, and happiness throughout life. Teens also need a strong supportive relationship with their parents. Supportive parents will provide structure and encouragement, guidance and love to their teen during this time of transition and change. It's important to remember and teach our teens the difference between quality and quantity. So often our children are chasing "likes" on social media apps, or they are measuring their worth through the number of friends they have or how often they are included in the mix with their friends. However, it's not the quantity that we should be thinking about, it is the quality. Even if your teen has one friend this is much better than having 200 friends who do not add to their development and self-esteem. It's important that teens take time to assess their relationships with friends as if you leave interactions with friends feeling drained, self-conscious or worse then you did before you hung out with them, they are likely not good for you. Since we are social beings, we are typically only as healthy as the company we keep or the environment we keep ourselves in.

How important are your friends to you? Do your friends empower you and build your self-esteem or make you feel better about yourself? Do your friends more often make you feel insecure, unwanted or unsuccessful? When you think of your friends you spend the most time with, are they performing academically, socially and emotionally the same as you? When you think of the last five conversations or social media exchanges you had with your friends, were they positive? Or Negative? Do you frequently complement your friends, or do they often compliment you?

N – Novelty. Teens seek out and create novel experiences to satisfy the increased activity of the reward circuits in their brain. They need new and creative ways to engage their minds, stimulate their senses, spark their thinking, and engage their bodies. As parents, we can work to help them find ways to live passionately and adventurously while teaching them to think through consequences of actions and reducing risk of harm. One way to do this is to engage the teen's creativity. In life we are constantly growing and changing. This places new demands on our brains and personality. As parents and educators, it's important to utilize the novelty seeking brains of teens through adding them in more conversations and opportunities to find solutions. So often it can be easier as adults to do things by our self, quickly and efficiently. However, allowing our teens to gradually increase their responsibility is good for them as it allows them to "fill their cup" in this critical area. In my experience the children who have greater breath in what they do and what they enjoy are much more resilient and happy children.

When life becomes too hectic or too monotonous it's important to keep a healthy balance of things you enjoy doing. Remind your teen regarding the simple things in life as when we grow old of life's natural pleasures, we set ourselves up for a world and reality where we have to constantly be entertained, stimulated or busy. Constantly seeking novelty can be detrimental to teens as their minds are constantly stimulated, however, they may not be achieving any more than they would if they took time to "smell the roses". Brain growth and development comes from learning how to regulate yourself, be at peace with silence and find time to balance yourself.

What are the three most interesting things in your life? What is an activity or hobby you can enjoy by yourself? What is an activity you do that excites you? What type of problems or situation do you find pleasure in solving? What type of activities or situations easily grab your attention? How often do you take alone time? Is it difficult for you to be alone with your own thoughts?

C. E.—Creative Exploration. Teens and tweens grow in their ability to think abstractly and problem solve, and they become better at using all the parts of their brain. For example, if you are experiencing a flood of emotion, an adolescent brain is now learning the ability to use reason to balance emotions and put out the fire.

At earlier ages children are not able to use different parts of their brain to calm or soothe themselves, so they use parents, adults or anything outside of themselves to make them feel better. However, when you become older, you can use your own thoughts to soothe you when you have an emotional experience. During this time teens reflect more on what they know and believe. As a result, they gain a new, and often ideal, perspective of how to impact the world around them. They ask questions and point out perceived injustices and discrepancies.

They also seek out novel solutions for the problems they perceive in their world, their home, and even in their parents. This offers a wonderful opportunity to talk and connect with your teen as you share ideas and perspectives in a calm, non- judgmental discussion. This is also a great time as parents to evaluate yourself and not become defensive when your children offer their views on what they see in you. This could be an opportunity to be self-reflective and improve. This is a perfect opportunity to work and grow together. Having a partner as oppose to and oppressor is much more affective at this age. It's imperative that parents create clear boundaries on how to communicate grievances and opinions as ultimately parents are still parents and deserve a certain level of politeness. Just like if you have a supervisor at work, even if you disagree, you must maintain a certain level of politeness.

How do you express your creativity? Do you feel you could be more creative in life? Is creativity important? Does your home life, school life, or work life allow you to express your creativity? How much energy are you or do you put into creative exploration? Do you feel you can perform age appropriate task at home? Do you have age appropriate responsibilities at home? Does your home offer you age appropriate opportunities to become part of the family? Is your role in your family changing? Would you like your role and responsibility to change?

Takeaway points:

Cultivate Discipline and Respect: There's a sweet spot and a comfort zone that we all have where we feel safe, seen, soothed and secure. In this growth zone we can make good decisions, respond to life as oppose to react, and develop and maintain healthy relationships with our families. This growth zone can be allusive for families as it involves work, choosing clean pain and a willingness to work on yourself individually. The first of the keys to setting up a successful environment for adolescent development is to teach and help children learn the ESSENCE of the time they are growing through. When you and your teen both understand the forces you are working with it creates a mutual understanding. As we just discussed these areas can be great gifts and they can also become problematic if left unrefined.

Talking and developing an understanding of what health looks like in the areas of emotional spark, social engagement, novelty and creative exploration will give both parents and teens a goal and starting point. When you have a goal and a starting point you have the recipe for balance as you will know when things are outside of what is expected. For example, if you notice the area of social engagement is out of balance as your son is focusing an imbalanced amount of time with his girlfriend and it is affecting other aspects of his life. You can bring the conversation back to what balance looks like in this area. This is where the work and the choice to choose clean pain comes in. If you remember clean pain is the pain that comes from choosing action that will ultimately lead to health and growth. As oppose to dirty pain, which is the pain that comes from ignoring, hiding or fighting the tough actions that should be taken. For example, talking to your son about the inordinate amount of time he spends with his girlfriend, no matter how upset, hurt and or passive aggressive he gets is choosing clean pain. Dirty pain would be ignoring, excusing or allowing the behavior to continue and thinking it will preserve a relationship. The later choice will ultimately lead to more hurt, pain and trauma. However, people often choose dirty pain as it saves you from hurting in the immediate. Clean pain is an investment for the future and when you come home after a long day, many people choose the dirty pain.

During these times mutual respect and having a structured way of communicating is important for families. This structure and routine can calm the adolescent brain and body as they will know what to expect and how to communicate in a somewhat changing power dynamic in the home. If you can imagine because the teen brain is flooded with emotional sparks, the desire to engage socially with peers and the ability to think creatively about how things should be changed, it may be difficult for them to have what is perceived as a judgment rendered on their choices and decision making. Just think if we had someone come into our lives and start to tell us how to live it. In order to take the sting out of being somewhat of a life consultant we have to set up situations that are safe for the teens developing ego. Ways to create safe home environments for teens are:

Adults self care: We must have room and space in our own nervous systems to be able to support our teens in regulating and managing their lives. Often as parents and caring, community members we seek to work and attempt to provide balance for teens when we are not regulated or balanced ourselves. When we work with teens, we are lending them our self-regulation skills as well as our nervous systems. Many times, people regulate themselves through using the people in their environment. It's important for parents to ensure they have a self-care routine that allows them to "pour out of their cup" so they can have free space to handle life situations without anger or judgment. Our children/youth need us to lend them our strength, calm, and reasoning skills as some situations cause these skills to go "offline" for some teens. If our cups are too full due to our own lives and trauma's, we have no emotional skills to lend them. This can leave our children/ youth feeling emotionally neglected and in a conflictual state. As parents grow with their children through adolescents this requires working on themselves and their own mental health. In order for parents to be free of judgment or overly emotional responses, they must first be in a place where they themselves are calm and regulated. We shape our children through our relationships and in order to change their behavior, we have to change our responses to our children.

Create opportunities for Independence: We must promote appropriate levels of autonomy for teens and use the great sparks of energy and life that is associated with the ESSESCE of adolescents. Creating opportunities for independence is healthy for the parent and teens as it builds trust and respect. Further, it allows teens to grow beyond the ceiling the parents and family provide for them. When opportunities for independence are denied it can be a recipe for resentment or undermine the teens confidence in the area of self-initiative. We should value our teens desire to create and build independent of us as this is what sharpens their skills for life.

Support teens in finding a new tribe: We must use our insight into the past and be aware of what could be driving our teens current behavior. This means we know the new influences in our teen's lives. One of the major transitions a teen must make is finding a new tribe. This is they will be looking for friends, elders and community members that align with their view of life and their direction and these people will likely not be directly associated with their family. To the greatest extent possible parents and guardians should strive to be part of the new tribe or have a understanding of who the new tribe is for their teen.

Create a trusted team or counsel: Having a team of individuals that meets regularly to discuss how things are going for the teen is a great way to show investment and create a village for the teen. We have all heard the African proverb "it takes a village to raise a child" and this is certainly true. Teens benefit from having a variety of people who support them and ensure things are on track. The team should consist of people that the teen trust, respects and or who has a skill set the teen would like to gain or admires. The team should be confidential and designed to empower the teen and not punish them. This is not a disciplinary team, rather a problem solving, strategy building team. Examples of members of the team could be a long-time teacher, parent(s), older sibling, pastor, and friends.

Having the perspective of other trusted people can help you build your insight into situations and a deep sense of connection. *Connection with other people, family in particular*, is protective, nurturing, and sustaining. Connection protects against challenges for teens, and it encourages more intimacy and continuing connection. Our teens need a deep sense of connection to their families, their higher power, nature, and the world of others around them.

Make healthy habits apart of the home: Building healthy habits will decrease the number of unsettling events you experience in your life. When you have healthy work habits, sleep habits and social communication habits it decreases the opportunity for minor challenges to become major. Since part of the ES-SE-N-CE of adolescence is creative exploration, teens will likely see ways and think of ways to help you structure your life and create healthy habits. If you can be open to this and become somewhat of a servant leader, this will make it more likely they will follow your lead and develop healthy habits. Go on the journey with them as if not this can and often does cause challenges and negative responses as the adage "do as I say and not as I do" is not functional.

Have a way to reward and consequence: Structure your home in a way that does not take away your ability to reward and consequence. When you give everything a way for free, such as buying things without them being earned, you are creating a behavioral orientation in your child that you or the world will not be able to maintain. This will leave them behaviorally maladapted and vulnerable in the world. Think of it like a job, if you were paid no matter how you performed the company would have no way to reward or consequence you. Sometimes our teens can work us into situations where we give them so much as we are choosing dirty pain. This means, we are selecting to appease them now, even though we know it is not teaching them the necessary skills or preparing them for future responsibilities. It's important that we safeguard our rewards and utilize them for shaping their behavior and holding them accountable for the growth they need to make. If we lose our power to reward and consequence it will be hard to shape their behavior and choices.

Summary:

It's my sincere hope that you enjoyed this book. It was my intention to provide knowledge, promote understanding and to empower families through conversation. Families are instrumental in the development of mental health skills and overall wellness. However, no one is perfect, so it's imperative that we seek to understand ourselves and the ones we love as it's through this understanding that we can grow in a healthy way. As a child I experience many environmental, systemic and familial situations that could be considered risk factors. However, it was the love, devotion and commitment of my family to work on themselves and communicate that allowed me to learn to love myself in a healthy way. I truly hope this book has inspired you and your family to choose "clean pain" and work on the challenges that will ultimately free you from present day or generational wounds.

CPSIA information can be obtained
at www.ICGtesting.com
Printed in the USA
FSHW021754221219
65367FS